What
Day Is It?

NEW ISLAND

Who gives a fuck

For everyone

Contents

Everybody is a poem

Everybody is a poem,
Every walk is a dance,
Every family is a drama,
Every chat's a performance.

Every recording is a film,
Texts are memoirs
    from the heart,
Every body is a poem,
Every limb's a work of art.

RAGE

Peak Rage

I'd reached peak rage,
Couldn't hold it all in.
I'd had it with parks and social distancing.

My thoughts and bad language
Leaked onto a page.
It made me feel better, felt released from a cage.

I shared it with friends,
It struck a chord with each one.
They all felt the longing, frustration and fun.

'Can I post on my Twitter?'
'Of course, Róisín, do!'
Replies and responses pinged in with 'me too'.

Simple words struck a chord.
I am no academic.
Is it safe to go viral in a global pandemic?

Poxy Park

Poxy park.
Poxy walks.
Let's just be silent.
I don't want to talk.

Poxy cold.
Poxy bench.
'Pick up your dog poo.'
The poxy stench.

Poxy bored.
It's time to go
Back poxy home.
Don't be so slow.

Poxy shop.
Poxy queue.
Hurry up!
I need the poxy loo.

Poxy telly.
Poxy news.
More advice
That'll just confuse.

Poxy clock.
Poxy bed.
Poxy worries
Fill my head.

Tomorrow,
please god, amen.
I'll wake up tired.
And do it all again.

Borrow Strength

I don't care if one summer he worked in your
    pub
Or cheered on the sidelines for the GAA club.
How dare you declare him a very nice chap;
What he did in that moment is evil, you SAP!

Fuck your boys' club descriptions, shut your big
    stupid mouth.
Your words they mean nothing, the truth has
    won out.
Instead, ask yourself, would you say all of these
    things,
If your girl was sat in that court circus ring?

Our sister, we're with you. We see you. We care.
We support you. We love you. We're going
    nowhere.

We walk alongside you, today and tomorrow,
While you build up your own, we have strength
    you can borrow.

LEARNING

SCHOOL TIMETABLE

SUBJECT	MONDAY	TUESDAY	WEDNESDAY	THURSDAY	FRIDAY
MATHS *TEACHER: MUM	SOFA	BED	PARK	KITCHEN	KITCHEN
ENGLISH	GARDEN	KITCHEN	T.V	BED	SOFA
IRISH	KITCHEN	SOFA	T.V	T.V	BED
ART	KITCHEN PARK	PARK	BED	GARDEN	BED
P.E	PARK	BED	YOUTUBE	TWINKLE	KITCHEN
SCIENCE	PLAYROOM	BED KITCHEN	YOUTUBE	SOFA	PARK
WELLBEING	✓	✓	✓	✓	✓

YouTube School

They'll learn off YouTube, won't they?
It's full of facts, I'm sure.

Along with all the Minecraft hacks,
Cat videos and bedroom raps.
Joe Wicks P.E. must fill the gap . . .

They might learn French,
Bonjour!

Homeschool Sofa

Today I homeschooled on the sofa,
They say you should do it on chairs.
You cannot take phone calls, no distractions at
    all,
They can tell by the work if you care.

English reading was highly successful,
History class went remarkably well.
In slippers and big fleecy PJs,
We took part in the class show-and-tell.

I do not get the fractions in *Busy at Maths*.
And Irish: COMPLETE wreck the head.

Today I homeschooled from the sofa.
Tomorrow I'll homeschool from bed.

Twinkle Isn't Teaching

Twinkle isn't teaching,
Seesaw isn't school.
And Joe Wicks in the kitchen
Is *not* P.E. you fool.

The sofa's not a school desk,
The laptop's not a book.
Tea and cake is not Little Break,
No hands up if you're stuck.

I'm not Miss Byrne, Miss Johnston,
Mr Sullivan or Mr Ryan.
That playroom's not a science lab
And the park is *not* yard time.

The alarm clock's not the school bell,
At 2, there's no school run.
There's no white board to calculate,
No friends to share the fun.

Assembly's done on Facebook,
Zoom hosts show-and-tell.
The best days of your life, they say.
Not this. It's fuckin' hell.

Midterm Breakdown

At last,
Put those bloody books away,
Leave the telly on all day.

Don't make the bed,
Leave it messed.
Don't clean your teeth,
Or bother to get dressed.

Send them out the back to play,
Hide the dirty clothes away.
Pull the blinds so you can't see
The mucky floors; cups stained with tea.

Stay up really late,
Drink all the gin.
Don't set your alarm for an early dawn swim.

'It'll be a bit easier,
Now the weather is warmer.'
Eat on the couch,
Stuff your face with a Korma.

Have a good cry
When no one's around.
Go on,
It's midterm breakdown.

Don't Take One Back, Take the Two

Don't take one back,
Please, take the two;
Just up to second class won't do.

The morning rush will still be a 'mare.
We'll dash back home, to sit and stare
At Seesaw on a bloody screen.
The child gone in is turning green
With envy at his sister here.
At home with me, she's not so clear
On complicated fifth class maths.
Because her homeschool teacher's CRAP!

Please, not just one back,
Take the set?

No?
OK. For now, I'll take whatever I can get.

Back to School Son

What day is it?
It's back to school,
No more kitchen classroom rules.
My son, our lessons are at an end,
Today you'll study with your friends.

I'll miss you,
But we'll both enjoy
Our time apart, my darling boy.

You'll play soccer in the yard,
Miss Cole will help with the maths that's hard.
At 2, I'll be there at the gates,
I'll hug you hard and kiss your face.

LONGING

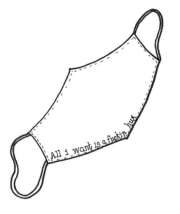

Touch Hunger

'I'm hungry.'
Child, I'm hungry too,
But I don't hunger the same as you.

You forage for chocolate, bikkies with jam.
Open and closing each press.

'PLEASE, DON'T SLAM!'

And while you're inside
Pulling the kitchen asunder.
I'm here, hungry too,
But mine is touch hunger.

What Day Is It?

What day is it?
Who gives a fuck.
I teach, I clean, I play, I cook.

This lockdown is a fuckin' pain.
Oh look, fuck sake,
Here comes the rain.

Another day, another park,
I'm wishing it would just get dark.

Please, no more fuckin' walks,
Or yoga, baking or art with chalk.
No meditation, fuck cold sea dips,
And fuck your healthy eating tips.

All I want is a fuckin' hug,
A chat, close up, with a massive mug
Of tea, none of this take-out crap.
I'd touch your hand; you'd slap my back,
We'd laugh and talk,
I'd share my cake,
We'd talk about who we think is fake.
We might say, 'Fuck it, stay out late.'
We'd grab an early-bird at 8.
We'd talk and chat and talk some more,
We'd link as we walk out the door.
On the bus, I'd text to say:
'My friend, I've had a lovely day.'

But FUCK.
What day is it?
I don't have a fuck.
I teach, I clean, I play, I cook . . .

Places I'd Rather Be

France,
Lounging by the sea.
In Mam and Dad's house
Drinking cups of tea.

BT's first floor,
Trying clothes I can't afford.
At a match, screaming
Because my team just scored.

Sitting in the middle
Of a table for six.
Overstaying my welcome
just for kicks.

In your house,
Not in mine.
In the church, lighting candles,
Saying prayers at the shrine.

Inside, anywhere,
Not out,
Dancing in a sweaty club,
In the pub, drinking stout.

With more than one other person,
Not just you and me,
In any of these places,
I'd much rather be.

Lockdown Crap

This lockdown's been a load of crap.
I walk the dog, I take a nap.

The job I had no longer there,
And no one seems to bleedin' care.

I had to move back with the ma,
I walk the streets, I've got no car.

All I want is to see the lads,
A pint or three, a chicken spice bag,
A football match, some training even.
'Did you hear about that fella Steven?
You know, the one from three doors down,
He couldn't take it; his body was found,
Well, my pal,
You know yourself,
When your head's not right,
You've to ask for help.'

So, I'm stuck here,
For another while I'd say.
I'm fuckin' lost.
What day's today?

Open Up the Future

Open up the future,
Switch on all the lights,
Unlock every bolted door,
It's time to reunite.

Open up the future,
Welcome us in inside,
Greetings with a gentle touch,
Will ease the great divide.

Open up the future, please.
Enough hurt we have withstood.
Open up the future, quick,
Before it shuts for good.

Let's Go Out When This Is All Over

Let's go out when this is all over,
Drive as far as we like, and we wish.
Visit your mam in Gleninagh,
Give her a big sloppy kiss.

Let's go out when this is all over,
Let's meet all our friends in one day,
In a small little place, where we sit face to face,
We'll eat in, no more takeaway.

CHEERS!
LET'S GET ABSOLUTELY
SOBER.

Let's go out when this is all over,
And buy all of the trends from the shops.
We'll queue for three hours in Zara.
For one little sparkly top.

Let's go out when this is all over.
Let's do then, what we cannot do now.

Let's go out when this is all over,
Go out and get utterly sober.

The Future Isn't Cancelled

Imagine the party we'll all have
In the future, when all this has passed.
There'll be drinking and singing and dancing,
Can't remember when we did it last.

We'll go wild to the beat of the music,
We'll mouth all the words to the songs,
We'll dance very close, embrace as we pose
For a selfie we'll save on our phones.

We'll go for Zaytoon after midnight,
We'll share our large Coke with a straw,
In the cab we'll plead with the driver:
'Can you turn up the music some more?'

Our tickets are dated 'the future',
I'll plan what I'll wear just because
The future, it hasn't been cancelled,
The future, it's just put on pause.

LOVE

Carpet or Tiles?

It's been so long since we've been on our own,
A teenager sits on our couch on her phone.

You shave your face, I pluck my chin
And wonder what clothes I might still fit in.
The leather trousers I bought in Dunnes Stores,
No chance will I squeeze into them anymore.
Maybe that dress from two Christmases gone?
The one you said made me look like 'yer wan'.

'Oh Jesus, wear anything,
Maybe look at the weather?
Whatever you're happy in,
Can't we just be together?'
(In t-shirt and jeans and your comfortable shoes,
We'll both look more gorgeous with the effects
    of the booze.)

'We won't be back late, just give me a call
If they have a bad dream, or they tumble and
    fall.'

'C'mon let's just go!
Shhhh! Don't slam the door,
Hold my hand,
Where's my keys? I won't wait anymore.'

'Where are you taking me? I'm not walking for
    miles.'
'Where do you fancy, carpet or tiles?'

Sufficiently Adequate

I'm sufficiently adequate,
I think you will see that I'll do.
You will never find anyone better than me,
I won't love no one like I love you.

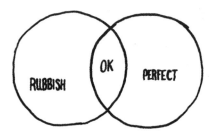

Emotional Distance

I don't want to be in your company,
It's easier to just stay away.
When you're feeling like this,
I see something's a miss.
So I'll be keeping my distance today.

Give My Feelings a Rest

That's it.
I'm off to bed.
I don't feel so great,
You're all wrecking me head.

No.
You've done nothing wrong,
I just need some quiet,
I won't have desert, I'm on that new diet.

Look.
It's been a long day,
My patience is wearing,
I need to lie down, my brain needs repairing.

So.
I'll go to bed early,
My head is a mess,
I'll just close my eyes and give my feelings a rest.

You Got Back Your Funny

There's a lightness about you,
Before now, it was missing.
There's mischief and charm,
and even some kissing.

You laugh at my jokes,
You reach out for my hand.
'How was your day?'
'It was great, sure I'm graaand!'

You lost some of your funny,
It was hard to stand by,
And see you despair, go to bed just to cry.

I loved you right through it,
How could I not?
You'd do it for me, you're all I've got.

Today, the sparkle is back,
Can't buy that with money.
I can see it, it's there, you got back your funny.

SELF

Overshare

I overshared.
You don't know me that well.
You might not get my jokes yet.
Or the stories I tell.

My constant proclaiming
Could be leaving you tired.
Don't worry, I know.
I'm a taste that's acquired.

One of Those Days

I had one of those days.
Sure, you know yourself,
The kind I know even the wine won't help.
To dull down the feeling of numbness inside,
I sat in the bathroom, I cried and I cried.

I ate all the biscuits,
I scrolled on my phone.
I roared at the kids:
'LEAVE EACH OTHER ALONE!'

I'll just call my friend,
That usually helps.

'Hello?
I've had one of those days.
Sure, you know yourself.'

Say My Name

Mother. Mammy. Ma.
I'm all of these three.
Mom. Mum. Mummy.
They also call me.

'Your Mum will collect you.'
'Your Mom's at the door.'
'Thanks for dinner, Mummy,
 Can we please have some more?'

'For god's sake behave,
 Or I'll tell your mother.'
'Let's just go, Ma.'
'No! Wait for your brother.'

My first name's gone missing,
I've searched each nook and cranny.
There's no need for it now.
I will answer to Mammy.

The Interview

'What am I?'
I said, getting it straight in my head.
She stared at me deeply and blankly.

'I'm a woman, a mother,
a friend, a childminder.'
(I wished I had titles more swanky.)

I cook every day,
My menu is vast.
But I'm not a chef,
Don't be so daft.

I give lessons on life
And correct all bad grammar.
But I'm not a teacher,
I don't have the manner.

I care for the sick,
Kiss everything better.
But I'm no Florence Nightingale.
(I never did get her.)

I clean top to bottom,
I wear gloves and a visor.
But I often miss spots,
I'm no sanitary advisor.
I wash five times a day,
Press 'anti-stain' and I'm set.
No one strips to their boxers,
In my launderette.

'What am I?'
I have trouble giving you a straight answer.
I'm an artist, a poet, a life-freelancer.

So, go ahead.
Edit out the roles you think are a bore.
I'm ALL of these things,
And I'm so many more.

Pretend We Never Met

You seen me,
Why did you not say hello?
We used to know each other,
Years and years ago.

I shared with you all of my secrets,
You let me cut off your long hair.
So why did you pretend
Like you didn't see me just there?

What will you do at the party?
Someone says, 'You two, have you met?'
Shake my hand and stare at me blankly,
And behave as though you forget?

All the fun and the jokes and the friendship
That we had, just past our teens.
I lent you all of my records,
Before me, you listened to Queen.

I borrowed your leather jacket,
I'm not sure it was ever returned.
Is that why you pretend you don't know me?
Or the snog with your fella confirmed

To you, that I couldn't be trusted?
I'm sorry, I've massive regrets.
We used to be friends a lifetime ago,
Now we pretend that we never met.

Meditation Cake

I tried to meditate today,
They say it clears the head.
It's not all it's cracked up to be,
So I had some cake instead.

You Know When Everything is Shit?

You know when everything is shit,
And you just want to wallow?
But you can't 'cos you've got maths to teach
And a curriculum to follow.

You know when you feel lonely,
But you want to be alone?
And the pictures of nice houses
keep you scrolling on your phone.

You know when you feel happy,
Bnd you want to share it out?
But you can't, you mustn't see your friends,
There's nobody about.

You know when you feel shit,
And you just want to wallow?
So, you wait till everyone's in bed,
A glass of red you swallow.

Richard

But he's my friend,
He knows me the best.
If I was a quiz,
He'd past the Me Test.

He knows my birth date,
My preferred colour lippie.
He gives me his coat,
When it gets a bit nippy.

So, you think he is just
A 'male counterpart',
But he's my very best friend
And he carries my heart.

Impressure

Impress your parents,
Impress your friends,
Impress your boss,
Do not offend.

Impress on Twitter,
Impress in school,
Impress on the job,
Abide by the rules.

Impress the coach,
Impress the trainer,
Impress the yogi,
Be kind to your neighbour.

Impress the barman,
Impress the guard,
Impress your new partner,
Get up the yard.

Each person you meet,
You must always impress,
And never let on,
Sometimes you feel a mess.

Remember to Be Kind to Yourself

Remember to be kind to yourself,
When your thoughts are beating you up.
Remember as well to be honest,
When you feel like just giving up.

It's OK to not look on the bright side
And ignore the linings of silver.
Sometimes the best thing is admit 'this is shit',
And flip the world your middle finger.

Shop the Look

Shop the look!
My weekend style.
The grass is always greener,
Perfect kitchen in Elephant's Breath,
And a house that is always cleaner.

White teeth.
Smiling kids,
Who wear what they are told.
Vegan healthy lunches.
A dog who's never bold.

Big car.
Shopping hauls.
Holidays to France.
Romantic dates with 'hubby'.
A family TikTok dance.

Scrolling.
Late night.
Unwashed with greasy hair.
Screen-grabbing for 'inspiration'.
More like compare and despair.

Fashion Week

Friday fits,
Saturday is too short,
Sunday is very tight,
Monday doesn't suit me,
Tuesday is oversized and too long,
Wednesday only works when it's layered with
    Thursday.

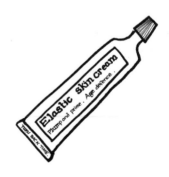

Elastic Skin

Anti-age,
Anti-aging power.
No more greys,
Tan in the shower.

Age defence,
Plump and prime.
Extra firming,
Turn back time.

'I haven't seen you for ages.
You look bloody fantastic.'
'Aw thanks. I'm using all of these creams
To keep my skin elastic.'

Since forever and ever,
We've been seduced by these potions.
Which claim to erase all our marks of emotions.

Our lines are our story,
Show our strength in our prime.
So let them grow freely,
Don't turn back the time.

Perfectly Imperfect

I'm perfectly imperfect.
I'm just like you, I am.

Look, here's my face, #nomakeup.
My body without a tan.

My clothes I 'shopped my closet',
Mother nature extended my hair.

See, I'm perfectly imperfect.
Stop! wait!
I'll just filter before I press share.

The News Today

WOMAN LEAVES IMMERSION ON.

They're painting their gates in Number 1.

Curry for dinner in 28.

Two doors down had a girl; baby Kate.

THE BINMAN CAME AT 12 NOT 2.

There's a special on steak in SuperValu.

My grey's growing out, my eyebrows are fuller.

Turns out, after all, pink isn't my colour.

THERE IS GREAT DRYING OUT,
    GOT THE TOWELS ON THE LINE.

Was going to hoover, but I didn't have time.

NEWS

THE BINMEN
CAME AT
12 NOT 2

HOOVERING
TO GO
AHEAD
TOMORROW

WELCOME
BABY
KATE

No Response Is a Response

No response is a response,
I hear you loud and clear.
I'm deafened by your silence,
Here you! Hear me. C'mere,

I'm not looking for solutions,
I don't even need advice,
Just let me know you heard me,
Some recognition would be nice.

I'll keep on checking in with you,
I have needs and wants,
I'll make you stop ignoring me,
'Cos no response, is a response.

Lonely Biscuit

Why have one, when you can have three?
One's not enough with a good cup of tea.

So if one is left, in the packet alone,
Put the kettle back on, sit and read on your
    phone.

It's a simple pleasure, you may as well risk it:
Enjoy one more cuppa and the last lonely
    biscuit.

6 a.m.'s the New Black

6 a.m.'s the new black,
Get up early so you can attack
The day ahead. Start feeling great!
Before the house gets up at 8.

Brew your coffee, organic, black.
Do hatha yoga, stretch out your back.
Knit your own muesli, sprinkle chai,
It'll keep you regular as the day goes by.

Watch the sunrise,
Be grateful, give thanks,
Hold a 30-minute plank.

Most mornings *I* get up at 6,
To sit in peace and watch Netflix.

Zoom Perfume

I put lipstick on, to take a phone call.

(No one else knew it was there at all.)
My face, on the screen, I thought and admired:
'A slick of red lippy stops me looking so tired.'

Washed and treated my hair,
Moisturised for an hour.
But those ruby red lips were my secret power.
And even though nobody saw,
I contoured like Kim, to define my slack jaw.

Listen, do whatever it is you have to do
To help make you feel the best version of you.
Slap a full face on to go to the shops,
Wear your Chanel to the butchers for chops.
Do whatever you need when the sluggishness
  looms.
Spritz your favourite perfume for your meeting
  on Zoom.

A Woman's Place

A woman's place is in the home,
Around it, and outside it.
Lean into work, like Sheryl said.
The laundry's done, she dried it.

Answer phones,
Review accounts
In time to make the tea.
Deliver babies,
Fix broken bones
And plaster bloody knees.

Drive the bus,
Cook the food,
Take the shopping order.
Write reviews,
Read the news,
Spend girly time with daughters.

Teach lessons,
Cut and style the hair,
Give partner strong support.
Stack the shelves,
Teach exercise,
Construct a blanket fort.

Encourage and enlighten,
Bake a birthday cake.
Sign off on that big project,
Ensure bedtime is 8.

Stand up in court and state a case,
Make coffee in a shop.
Be home in time for pick up,
Clean the kitchen with a mop.

A woman's place is everywhere.
Like God, she's omnipresent.
She splits herself in pieces,
At times it's quite unpleasant.

Safety Stocktake

Before I leave for home
I conduct a safety stocktake.
An inventory of sorts
for my own wellbeing's sake.

My phone is hidden deep
But it's always close to hand.
My keys are in my fist
As I'm walking up the strand.

I check left and right and left again,
I zigzag up the road,
Avoiding who I think I should;
A peculiar safe cross code.

Each step I take is speedy,
My bag is slung real tight.
I changed my shoes before I left
In case I got a fright.

'Nearly there,' I text you quick.
I take a slower pace,
Relax my grip and take a breath,

I've won the safety race.

Leggings

My clothes have no buttons,
My uniform is activewear:
With a full face of make up
And big blow-dried hair.

When I pull on my leggings,
I feel twisty and bendy.
My dress code by day:
Glam yoga class attendee.

They're power high-waisted,
lift and sculpting my bum.
No matter what day it is,
I'm dressed ready to run.

Even though, I admit,
I'm just off to the shops,
I feel athletic and sporty
Buying wine by the box.

I wore leggings for dinner,
Meatballs with spaghetti;
Changed into my blue ones,
for Pilates with Betty.

'Can you see my knickers?
These ones are so stretchy.
You sure they're not see through?
The cheap ones are sketchy.'

It's years since I was
V.I.P. at the gym.
Now wearing my leggings,
I feel sporty and trim.

Every day of the week,
There's no style evolution.
I wear 'hoody and leggings':
My wardrobe solution.

Poet Idol

For Róisín

I want to be your poet idol,
You've been my Simon Cowell.
I'll put my thoughts on paper, mugs,
and souvenir tea towels.

I'm no One Direction,
Behan or James Joyce,
But your rallying motivation
has helped me find my voice.

HIM

Get Up the Yard

Get up the yard,
Go out and play,
You can't stay in all day each day.

Stand up straight,
Pronounce your words,
Wear nice clothes or you won't get birds.

Work your balls off,
Save some cash,
Don't get mixed up in drink and hash.

Keep your job.
Hand up to your ma,
Go joyridin' with your mates in a car.

Get up, sign on,
Don't miss your slot,
Don't lose your temper with your mot.

Fix up, stand straight,
Try not to scag,
Find a safe place for your sleeping bag.

Get up the yard,
One final time,
Just one little hit, another line.

I Love You, Ma

'I love you, Ma.'
'I love you too.'
What I'd give,
To put my arms 'round you
Today, or any day this year.

I see your smile, it's really clear.
You broke my heart
And made a mess.
No need for flowers
Or a fancy dress

Today or any day
I guess,
I'd love a hug,
No more no less.

ELDERS

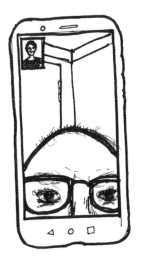

This Time Last Year

This time last year we were precious,
We were told to cocoon every day.
A kiss through the glass,
Can't see your face with that mask.
'Please God bring our jab quick,' we prayed.

All I want is a sloppy kiss
From my girl and the grandkids.
Oh Jesus, I miss
The feeling of somebody holding my hand.
It's just not the same when they all have to stand
At the end of the garden in the rain and the
    cold.
'Ah god, come on in.'
'NO, Dad, don't be so bold.'

And as for them WhatsApps
I can't hear a thing.
'Dad. DAD! PLUG. YOUR. HEARING. AID. IN.'

Your mother keeps busy with walking and
    dance,
On her exercise bike today, she cycled to France.
Jaysus wept, even my garden I'm beginning to
    hate.
But, this time last year we were precious.
Now, we just have to wait.

Kevin

We touch the glass,
He's in the bed.
His daughter gently strokes his head.

We made a banner, just to say:
'We think of you every single day.'
He lifts his hand, gives us a wave,
We think of all the love he gave
To us and everyone he met.
'He can hear each word we say,' I bet.

In his hand, the pocket hug
We made last week to show we could
Connect, and keep him safe from harm.
He settles back, she strokes his arm.
'Let's go now, he's tired,' she says.

We touch the glass, he's in the bed.

PARTY

MUSIC TO LOCKDOWN TO 0290-1848

DOUBLE CD

THE LOVERS

ROY ORBISON - ONLY THE LONELY

THE POLICE - DON'T STAND SO CLOSE TO ME

IRON MAIDEN - VIRUS

MICHAEL BUBLÉ - HOME

HALL AND OATES - OUT OF TOUCH

DIONNE WARWICK - WALK ON BY

SOUL II SOUL - BACK TO LIFE

NIRVANA - STAY AWAY

PRINCE - KISS

HEART - ALONE

MADNESS - OUR HOUSE

NOW 3 Lockdown

THIS WHAT I CALL

FLEETWOOD MAC - BIG LOVE

DIANA ROSS - REACH OUT AND TOUCH

MADONNA - HOLIDAY

GEORGE MICHAEL - FREEDOM

DIRE STRAITS - WALK OF LIFE

PINK FLOYD - WISH YOU WERE HERE

ELVIS PRESLEY - JAILHOUSE ROCK

THE PROCLAIMERS - I'M GONNA BE (500 MILES)

BLONDIE - IN THE FLESH

EMINEM - CLEANING OUT MY CLOSET

QUEEN - I WANT TO BREAK FREE

BLINK 182 - "I MISS YOU"

RUN DMC - WALK THIS WAY

FT I - RISE

EVERYTHING BUT THE GIRL - MISSING

THE FALL - REPETITION

ARCTIC MONKEYS - THIS HOUSE IS A CIRCUS

YEAH YEAH YEAHS - DESPAIR

JOE JACKSON - STEPPIN' OUT

L.C.D SOUNDSYSTEM

IGGY POP - J'M

JOY DIVISION

BONUS FACE MASK

Supermarket Disco

I disco in the supermarket,
I rave in fresh food aisles,
Self-service is my dance floor,
I bust all my dancing styles.

Bowie at the bakery,
Moloko in the queue,
Daft Punk around the frozen foods,
At cold meats: Don't Go Yazoo.

Will I ever club again,
Wave my hands up in the air?
For now, I'll dance in SuperValu,
They play the best tunes there.

Kitchen Disco

This kitchen was for dancing,
But that was long ago.
Today it is a classroom,
We're learning as we go.

An office and a meeting room,
A science lab and gym.
On Wednesday's Zoom assembly,
We learned to sing a hymn.

At Monday's art, we made a mess,
The floor was freshly mopped.
This kitchen *is* for dancing,
The music hasn't stopped.

Acknowledgements

Until January 2021, I'd never written a poem before. And I've never written acknowledgements, so I had to Google 'book acknowledgements' to see what it is I should include. Turns out it's a 'way to display your appreciation to everyone who helped with your book'. So here goes . . .

Thank you Roisín Ingle, Faith O'Grady and to the exceptional team at New Island. Thank you for giving me the chance to share these poems and drawings.

Thank you Mam and Dad, for taking all of my life's adventures in your stride and loving me through all of it.

Thank you Lesley, Richard and Brenda, for listening to my constant comploaning. Thanks to my secret keepers: trusted and loved friends and family. To Cecelia, thank you for the constant encouragement from afar.

Most of all, thank you to Austin, Willow and Theo, the best things about me are you three. I love you so much.

And to you reading this, thank you for finding this book and reading my poems.

See, we're not really strangers, are we?

WHAT DAY IS IT?
First published in 2021 by
New Island Books
Glenshesk House
10 Richview Office Park
Clonskeagh
Dublin D14 V8C4
Republic of Ireland
www.newisland.ie

Print ISBN: 978-1-84840-827-2
eBook ISBN: 978-1-84840-828-9

Typesetting and cover design by New Island Books
Printed by PlusPrint, Dublin
New Island Books is a member of Publishing Ireland

10 9 8 7 6 5 4 3 2 1